Rock, Rhythm and Rag

BOOK ONE

PIANO SOLOS

by Melvin Stecher, Norman Horowitz
and Claire Gordon

STECHER &
HOROWITZ

S&H

PIANO LIBRARY

ISBN 978-0-7935-6413-2

G. SCHIRMER, Inc.

DISTRIBUTED BY

HAL•LEONARD®
CORPORATION
7777 W. BLUEMOUND RD. P.O. BOX 13819 MILWAUKEE, WI 53213

JACK RABBIT JUMP

Playfully, with a bounce

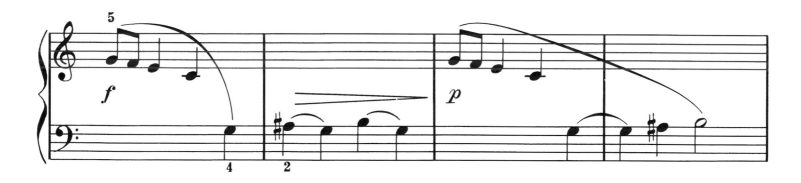

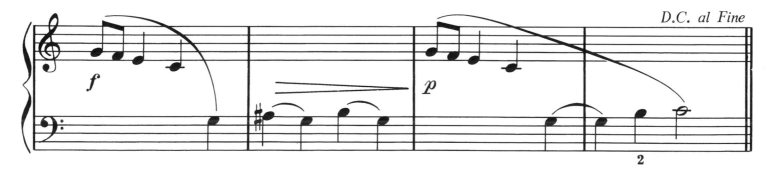

BUMBLE BEE BOOGIE

With a steady beat

SKY BLUES

Rather slow and singing

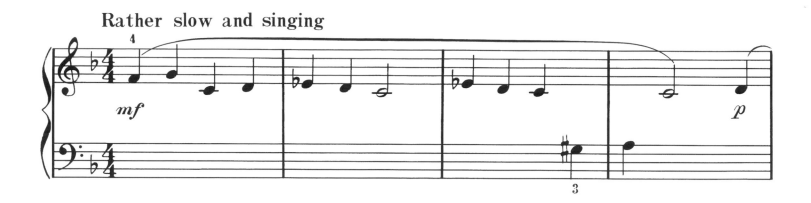

ROCK CANDY

RIVERBOAT RAG

With a ragtime bounce

MY SHADOW AND ME

With an easy swing

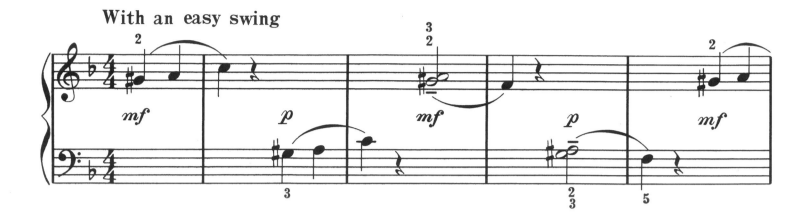

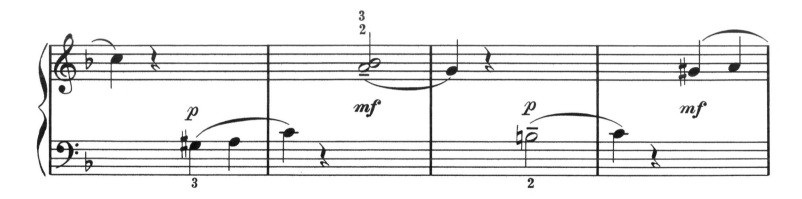

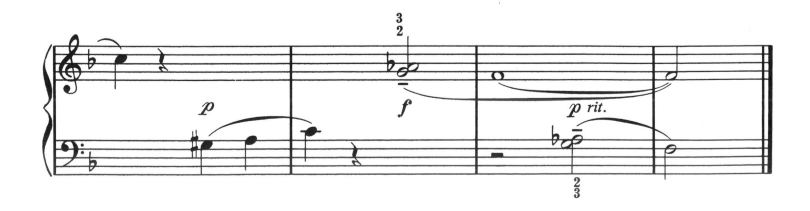

MARY'S LITTLE LAMB CHOP

Snappy and happy

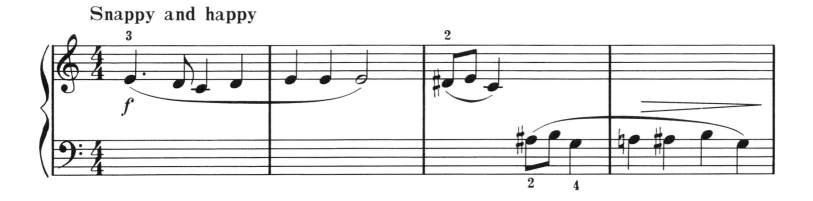

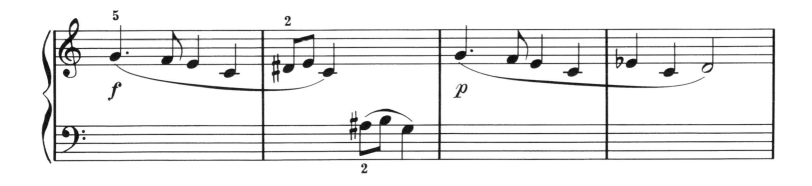

ROCKY ROAD

Solid and rocky

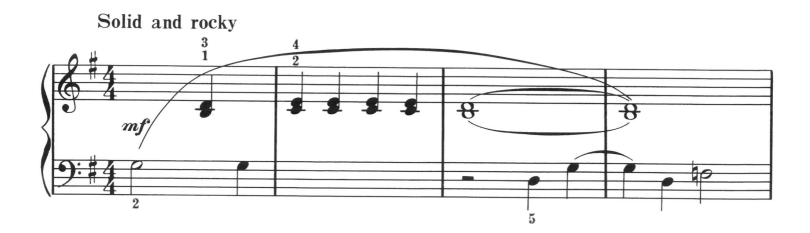

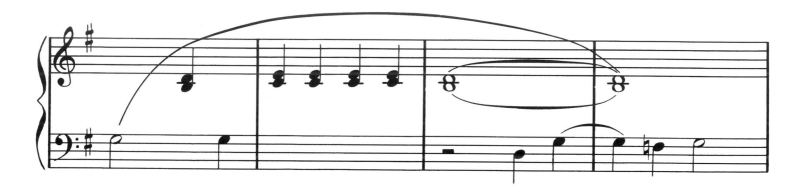

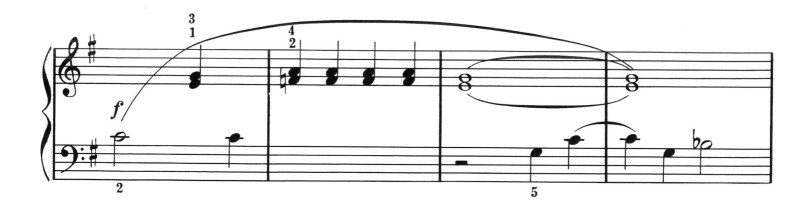

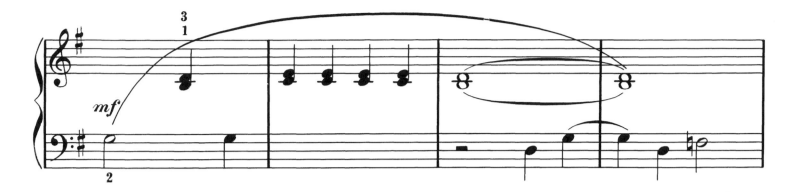

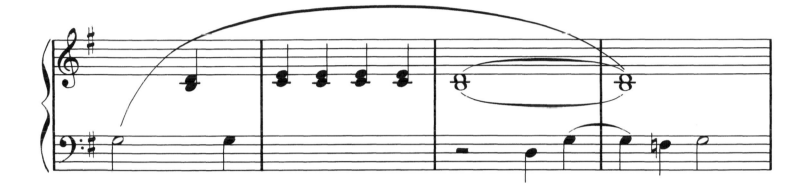

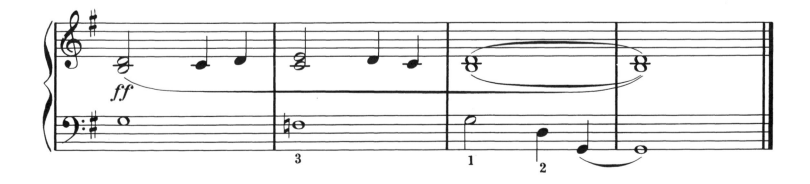

RAG-A-MUFFIN

Moderate rag tempo

SPACE ROCK

With a strong rock beat

DENIM BLUES

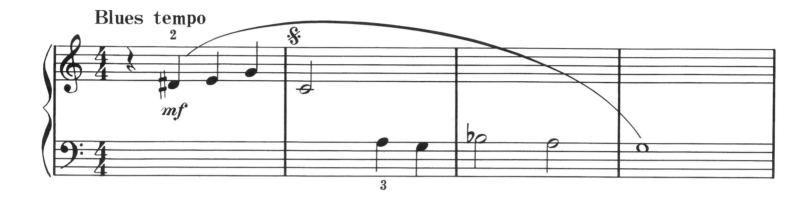

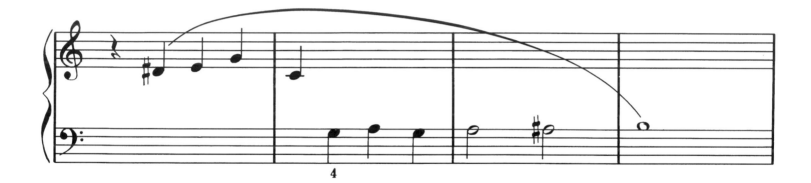

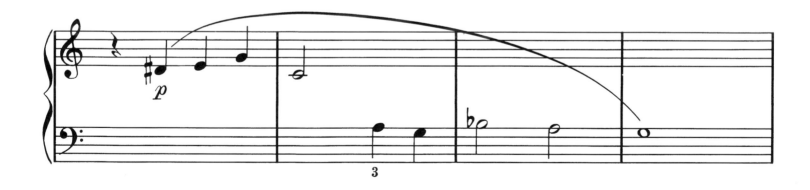

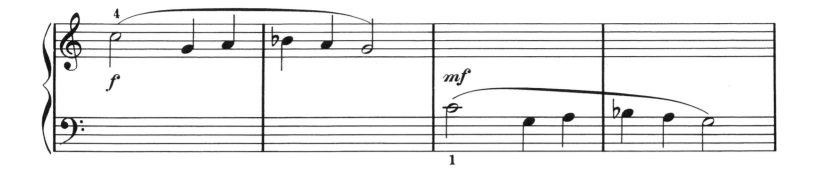

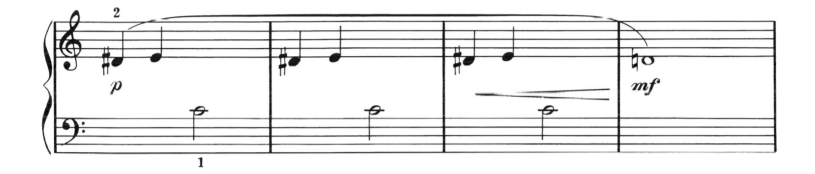

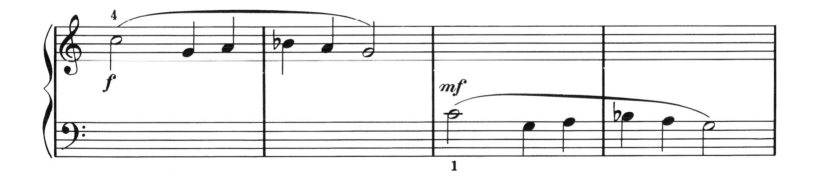

JAZZMOBILE

Rolling along

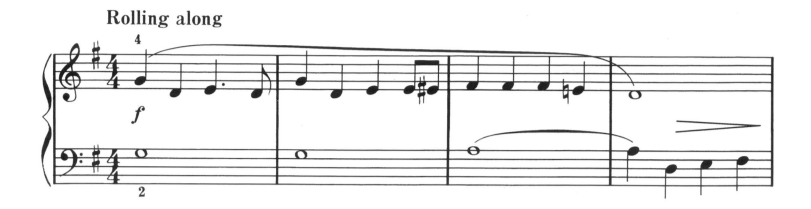

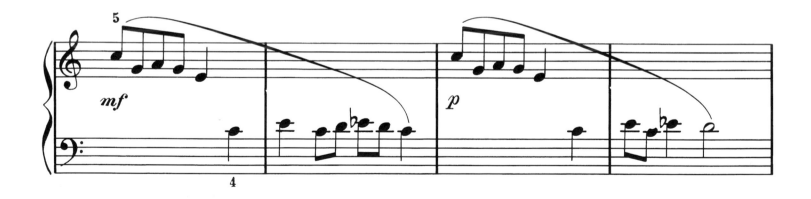

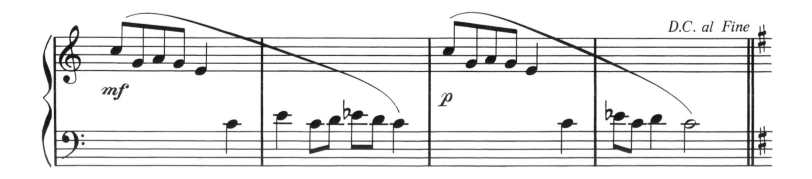